CHICO
and the
PATIENCE of a BANANA

by Peter Di Lisi
illustrated by Brant David

AuthorHouse™
1663 Liberty Drive
Bloomington, IN 47403
www.authorhouse.com
Phone: 1 (800) 839-8640

© 2018 Peter Di Lisi. All rights reserved.

No part of this book may be reproduced, stored in a retrieval system,
or transmitted by any means without the written permission of the author.

Published by AuthorHouse 02/15/2018

ISBN: 978-1-5462-2968-1 (sc)
ISBN: 978-1-5462-2967-4 (e)

Library of Congress Control Number: 2018902100

Print information available on the last page.

Any people depicted in stock imagery provided by Getty Images are models,
and such images are being used for illustrative purposes only.
Certain stock imagery © Getty Images.

This book is printed on acid-free paper.

Because of the dynamic nature of the Internet, any web addresses or
links contained in this book may have changed since publication and may
no longer be valid. The views expressed in this work are solely those
of the author and do not necessarily reflect the views of the publisher,
and the publisher hereby disclaims any responsibility for them.

CHICO
and the
PATIENCE of a BANANA

Our story begins with Chico the monkey, enjoying the bright blue sky.
As Chico was looking up he noticed a huge banana in a tree way up high.

Chico started getting excited, as he could not believe what he could see.
How in the world was he going to get that banana, up in that very tall tree?

Chico thought he could go
ahead and just climb it,
getting that banana would be no problem at all.
Chico started climbing up that tree,
but before he knew it he started to fall!

That trees bark was just too slippery,
Chico could not get a very good grip.
Every time Chico started climbing up that tree,
his hands would begin to slip.

Chico sat at the bottom
of that tree, as he heard a
little voice say.
"That banana is not quite
ready yet my friend,
you should go have fun and play".

Chico kept on trying and trying,
He didn't want to listen to what
that little voice had said.
He knew he could get that
banana if he wanted to,
he would just have to come up
with a clever plan instead.

Chico looked up at that great big banana,
with energy and a whole lot of hope.
Chico started gathering up some tree vines,
that he could use as a very long rope.

Chico spun that rope as
fast as he could,
to make sure he could get that
rope nice and high.

But Chico overestimated the
distance of that banana,
and the rope just kept swinging
right on by.

As Chico sat there tangled in the vines,
he once again heard the little voice say.
"That banana is not ready to come down my friend,
you should go and come back another day."

But Chico was feeling very smart,
so he thought he could give it another try.
Maybe making some wings out of leaves he thought,
and like a bird fly up nice and high.

Chico did a great job making some wings,
he was on his way up with a huge flapping sound!
But it was harder then he thought to control his direction,
as he crashed into the tree before hitting the ground.

Chico's head was spinning like crazy,
as he once again heard that little voice say.
"I am telling you for your own good my friend,
just go home and come back another day."

Chico was determined to have that banana,
waiting was just not an option in his eyes.
He wasn't willing to give up so easy,
and he could not help but give it a few more tries.

After trying and trying to get that banana,
and each time having no luck at all.
Chico looked up and accepted the fact,
that he will just have to wait for that banana to fall.

He heard that little voice a little louder this time, saying "you were trying just way too soon."

Chico looked around for were the voice was coming from, and he noticed a butterfly coming out of a cocoon.

"Sometimes you need to take your time"
she said "rushing will get
you nowhere really fast.
Just have a little patience relaxing in
the moment, and that time of waiting will
soon be in the past.

There is really no reason to rush things,
if you really want something just
keep it in your sight."
As the butterfly opened-up her wings
widely, with a big smile she began
to take flight.

The butterfly flew nice and high,
landing on that huge banana up
in the tree.
She barely needed to put any pressure
on it, to allow that banana to
become free.

Chico the monkey caught that banana,
he could not believe he finally had it in his hand.
He was very happy to be able to get it,
even though it did not come as fast as he had planned.

The banana just needed some time to become ripe,
no matter what Chico did it wouldn't have helped him one bit.
Sometimes waiting for the right moment to get something,
patience seems to be the perfect fit.

"When things are not going as fast as you like,
just have patience and you will soon see.
Most great things take a little time to come,
there is no reason to rush what will soon be."
by Peter Di Lisi
illustrated by Brant David

About the Author

Ever since Peter Di Lisi was young, he loved using his imagination in just about everything he did. He is now putting his imagination into a series of children's books that have lovable characters along with some great morals, and told in a fun upbeat rhyming style.

Peter grew up in the small town of Port Perry and has since traveled near and far incorporating things he has learned in life to inspire all his books. The Chico series started when he was working in an elementary school, and the kids fell in love with a puppet monkey named Chico that Peter had in his magic act that he did for the school. After the first story was written Peter quickly started thinking of other adventurers that Chico the monkey would have and that the children could learn from.

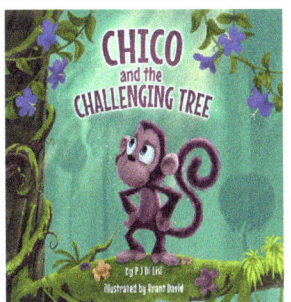

Look for these titles and more
peterdilisi.com

CPSIA information can be obtained
at www.ICGtesting.com
Printed in the USA
LVHW07s2240220818
587687LV00004B/4/P